YOU ARE YOUR OWN SUCCESS

PREFACE

Dear Reader,

"You Are Your Own Success" was written to inspire people that may have a vision, but don't know how to start working on their vision. This book will help guide you to learn how to trust your journey and how to envision what you can't see beyond where you are right now.

You have to trust that where you are right now is based only on what you know at this current moment. Once you begin to see the bigger picture, things will start to surface.

I started as young as twelve-years-old, braiding hair on my mother's porch. Maybe you are younger or older, but success doesn't have an age limit. Limiting yourself is a state of mind, and I'm ready to help you defeat those limited thoughts.

The first step in the process is "Remind yourself to Start."

Introduction

Where you are right now is exactly where you should be in order to position yourself for the next level in your life. We can get discouraged so quickly about our future, that disappointment can cause us to move like turtles in the present moment toward our goals. We can't cheat the hustle; it's a universal law. If you're given something before you are ready for it, you will spend many years trying to appreciate it.

Working toward what you want is the best gift you can give to yourself. It allows you to have a testimony that you can share with someone else. Your testimony can help others understand what they may be going through is just temporary, and your story may prevent that person from going down that same path.

Stop feeling stuck; we all get discouraged at some point. Teaching you to avoid staying stuck is the point of me writing this book.

What if I had stopped working toward my goals and thought that was it for my life? We were created to climb and not settle. You can be the best at whatever your passion is inside you. Take some time out to read books on success stories; most of them will have testimonies just like yours. You will realize their success story was simply of someone that did not give up.

One moment of me trusting myself earned me income at an early age. This was something most young girls living on the projects wasn't familiar with accomplishing. Where I lived, many people would lose their life, drugs were taking over the neighborhoods, and some teen girls were getting pregnant at a young age. I was a part of the environment, but not in the mix. I had friends and we all were different in our own way; yet alike at the same time.

As much as I liked hanging out, I also loved braiding hair. I spent most evenings braiding hair after school and on weekends; whenever I could, I would. I wasn't told not to braid hair, but I got yelled at a lot for braiding hair in the living room, which is still funny until this day because I proceeded to braid hair on the porch because no one was going to stop me.

My friends would come join me so that made it easy to focus, I wasn't missing out on anything. I also realized I didn't have as much enthusiasm about school as everyone else did, so it was rough getting up and pretending I wanted to be there. I had all the latest clothes and shoes. My aunt would have it laid out on the bed.

Chapter 1

"I Have to Get Out"

Telling myself, "I have to get out" was the starting point of my life. In 2009, I decided to go back to hair school for the third time around. Yes, three times! This is why I can't stress enough that you are your own success. After returning to school, for some reason I knew this was going to be the last time.

I said to myself, "I'm going to finish this time around." This was the era where Myspace was very popular and I wasn't familiar with it, but one of my coworker's was. I worked at a local hospital during this time, and was only doing hair at home. Even though I loved my job in the medical field, I didn't think it was the career that could help in paying my bills.

My coworker decided I should make a Myspace page to promote my work. Well, social media won because more people were able to see my work, and that meant more clients to service. In the back of my mind, all this sounded good but, I had bills to pay and a daughter that depended on me. My dilemma was not only if I quit my job, I would have to worry about bills, but how would I provide for my child? She wasn't a kid that wanted all the material things, so that made life a little easier. I got my Myspace page not realizing it was the start of a trend for me. My uncle called me *Trendsetta*, he said the "er" on the end of Trendsetter stood for everyone and he saw something different in me. So just adding an "A" on the end of the name brought life to my brand, and I had to single myself out as the *Trendsetta*.

Tip:

- "Your beginning is not your end."

Chapter 2

"I Left My Job"

I left my job at the hospital for another job. That didn't turn out well because I had a charge on my background that caused me to be ineligible for the new job. When I received the phone call on that morning telling me I didn't get the job, I thought that had to be the worst call to receive at that time. At least that's what I thought.

On the same morning I received the call that I wouldn't be hired, I heard loud screams coming from my neighbor. She was yelling at the top of her lungs, and since I couldn't sleep the disappointment off anyway, I decided to check on her. When I got up to see what was going on, at that very moment, I didn't know that my life would change forever. I didn't go to school to become a nurse. I realized I went to school for this very moment; her baby would need CPR. I performed CPR on her infant over and over again. But, we lost her - "My Angel." After this tragedy was when I knew I couldn't be a nurse; my poor heart ached. I knew at that very moment all of this was happening for a reason. All of this happened, including me leaving my job, because it was the start to me believing in my own success, and that I am my own success.

Later, I went to school full time and styled hair around my schedule. I was living in a low-income apartment and was able to manage my life around my daughter and my bills. In school I became a freak for knowledge on what to do after I graduated. I had already found a building to work in and enough clients to start off. But wait! No one just comes out of school and goes to work in a salon alone?

Tips:
- "The end of something, isn't always a finished project."
- "Never be afraid to leap."

Chapter 3

"I Finished School"

After three times of doubting myself and neglecting my gift, I finally finished school! I was so pleased with myself at that moment, you would've thought I won a million dollars! This didn't leave me feeling like it was over, I knew I had more to do. There were more goals to reach in order for me to be an example for my daughter. I named her *Unique,* she's been through all of this with me. I know she has triple the knowledge of what I've been able to expose her to.

I went on to take my test to become a licensed cosmetologist in the state of South Carolina. Initially, I didn't have the funds to take my test. Only because I forgot the one thing to always remember - "I am my own success and my own check." I started advertising on Myspace, and Facebook had just become a new platform for me at this point. This is when I started posting pictures on both sites and from there I was being contacted for bookings through both platforms. I booked over twenty appointments and had more than enough money to go to take my test.

I sent off my paper work and got a date scheduled. One of my friends volunteered to take me, but we ran into a problem at the hotel. Little did I know, we had issues with the hotel and transportation, and by the time I got there, it was too late to take the test.

I was discouraged, but I didn't give up. I contacted another young lady I went to school with and she informed me of another date. I put in a request for that date and I was accepted. I decided to go with my classmate to take the state board exams, and my friend wouldn't be driving me this time; my uncle took us.

As the time got closer, I checked my bag that I had set up for state board and guess what, I was missing some important items! Not only was that hotel change a disaster at the same time it was a blessing. Every situation that seems to be the worst isn't always as it seems. I encourage everyone to look at the bigger picture and don't give up. "If you don't know, ask."

Once you discover your gift, life changes you and you just can't walk away. You may receive tests to prepare you for a greater tomorrow but, your gift is connected to you for a purpose. You can do a hundred different things but your gift will always serve as a reminder of your success; I'm here to tell you. You can't negate your gift, you can waste it, but it can't be denied. If your dream is to be a stylist, go to hair shows, take classes, fix your family and friends hair. I'm basically saying prepare!
I'm finally going to take my test!

Tips:

- "Stay relevant."
- "There's no specific number of tries you need to hit a goal."

Chapter 4

"I Passed My Cosmetology Test"

I am now licensed in the state of South Carolina and I'm a cosmetologist! I went straight into the salon alone, just like I envisioned. I planned all of this in cosmetology school. I wrote a plan and stood by my dreams. I prayed for my day and went straight into the salon. I thought I had it all figured out, everyone from the kitchen was going to follow me to the salon. Well, I figured it wrong and I only had seven clients that followed.

Once again, I felt lost and it seemed like I wasted my time. But hold up, I forgot I am my own success! I went back to what I knew I was best at and went on social media, which was all I had utilized as advertisement, along with the word-of-mouth from my supporters. I'm here to tell you, "YOU ARE YOUR OWN SUCCESS." That month alone, coming straight out of cosmetology school into a salon own my own, I made $6500. That may seem like a small amount, but I knew my numbers and I thought it was excellent!

I want everyone who is thinking of stepping out and starting their own career to know that it is possible, and everything will be ok. I didn't drag you all through all of my hardships just to talk. I explained all of this to let you know that obstacles will happen, even until the day we leave this earth. My point is to get you to understand that everything you need is already in you, and no one can take that from you; it's yours. Also, education is one of the keys to success. Education is the foundation.

I studied my career and social media in school and I had no idea the effect I had on people. I didn't know what you put out is what folks will accept, but it worked. Now I want you to stop thinking that you need money to start. I just told you, you are your own check and someone is waiting on the gift you're holding back to surface. Someone is waiting to hear your story so they can start just like you. Someone has been watching you.

Everything is going well in the salon, but now I'm moving. I've completed my time on low income and I'm ready to take a step up and decided to move. The feeling of doing things right was overwhelming. My daughter is doing great in school and I'm doing great in my career.

I would like to give the titles of seven books that kept me going:

"Never Get Comfortable"

"The Finale is a Start for a Goaldigger"

"The Bible"

"48 Laws of Power"

"Secrets of the Millionaire Mind"

"Act Like a Success, Think Like a Success"

"Million Dollar Stylist"

Chapter 5

I Wanted to Work

I moved and got that feeling again of going back into the corporate world to give nursing another chance. However, I began to realize, we have to stay focused on what it is we have set out to do. If you don't know what to do, pray about it and find a mentor. Praying and speaking with a mentor can save you a whole lot of money and frustration.

I tried working again and of course it didn't work because that was not my passion. It's just another way to make money and that's cool, but there's nothing more fulling than living out your own dreams. I took a step back and thought things over. I am my own success so what better way to make more money than to use myself to do it.

Tips:

- Remember Why You started"
- Write Down Your Vision
- Find A Mentor

I want to take a break for you to think about some things. I want you to list five reasons you need a mentor.

1.
2.
3.
4.
5.

I also wanted to include a copy of my Real Vision Goals:

Date: 12-11-13

- Peace, strength and wisdom
- to remain a healthy relationship w/daughter
- Good Health
- To fulfill the needs in church
- Knowledge to run my home and business.
- 6 Figures
- Traveling Opportunities
- Several salon locations
- Salon instructor
- Range Rover

Chapter 6

"I Made My Vision Clear"

I wrote my vision down, not knowing that I would actually see it unfold; one by one, and not in the same order. I had to prepare myself for every step; and I also took classes. My motto is, "I'm a student first." To advance in anything you first need to be a student. I created a magazine, I had a phenomenal hair show and staged lots of photoshoots. I thought of ways everyday to brand myself and I had a good support system when it came to my ideas and future goals.

I held small classes in the salon and offered one-on-one sessions. "I am my own success" is my slogan. I believe every letter of this phrase. I am a living witness that your gift will make room for you. He gives seed to the sower.

You are your own check. I could go get a job or I could allow my gifts to blossom. I could wait on someone to hand me a paycheck or I could let my gifts pay me.

Once you see the bigger picture you can't stop. You will begin to create idea after idea and you will start to make better decisions. Most importantly, you will be leading the way for other stylists or anyone else that wants their own business, or those who just want to let go and follow their dreams.

My goal with this book is to provide you with insight of a young lady that wanted a check, not realizing all the dreams within her would pave the way. Nothing is easy and staying focused isn't any easier, but the job must get done. Go out with "joy" do not lose your peace.

Chapter 7

"I Needed to Brand Myself"

A few chapters ago, I talked about *Trendsetta* and how I wanted to be different, but now I needed to brand myself again. So this time, I knew I needed to find a brand that would separate me from the pack. I asked myself, "What I wanted my next five years to be like?"

I thought of all the styles I did and what I wanted my clients and future clients to expect. I love doing short hairstyles and I'm also a versatile stylist. I have a strong passion for healthy, rich looking styles. I love to see women embracing their hair and I love natural rich looking weaves.

Tips:

- You must add value.
- Ask yourself, "What's Your Passion?"

Chapter 8

"I Branded *StyleRich*"

I thought long and hard on this name because I know rich is rich no matter what. I said to myself, "if I use rich, I better be ready to make my styles, *Style Rich.*" I wasn't afraid at all because I knew this was based on my passion, and I couldn't go wrong doing what I loved to do. I studied daily on ways to keep my styles rich. I love this name and I needed my clients and future clients to feel this the moment they looked at my styles.

I also needed them to know who is behind *StyleRich* and why. I thought this is the time to make it happen, and I had to remember that, *I'm my own success.* Attraction is the most powerful thing in the world.

Chapter 9

"I Have Products"

I thought of ways to let others know who is behind *StyleRich*. I wanted to do things in state and out of state. But who is *StyleRich* and who should trust *StyleRich*? Why do my styles need to be rich? I placed S*tyleRich* on multiple items and I change my social media names, business cards, websites and first, but definitely not last, my clients' hair. This was "The Big Goal" and the meaning behind the name and the success behind my accomplishments.

I'm now branded as *StyleRich*. All of this was done through long nights, sickness, classes, and reading book after book. But, it was all worth it. But you have to remember it's in you and no one will have a vision like you - NOBODY can copy your purpose/platform/product.

Tip

- Think of Branding Products

I want you to think of five Promotional items you could create for your business.

1.

2.

3.

4.

5.

Chapter 10

"I Am the Proud Owner of Style Rich Salon"

After six years of hard work and dedication I can breathe about my past experiences and I can guarantee you that, *YOU ARE YOUR OWN SUCCESS!"*

Never allow anything to make you think or feel less than what you are. You'll experience many trials, but you'll save yourself a lot of wasted time learning from the experience of another.

I leave you with this message and I'm expecting you to go out and GET IT!

DEDICATIONS

Unique,

      This book is dedicate to you. I want to thank you for not being a headache (smile). I just appreciate you through all my trials and tribulations. I could not ask for a more supportive daughter. We've grown so much with each other. I can only imagine what you have in store for me to see. I've watched you from a seed to a Unique Flower and I enjoy watching you blossom.

Love,
Mom

Barbie,

      You are the mother to me and my mother and we enjoy fighting over you. You are an angel sent from above that got to walk this earth in flesh. I'm honored to be among you and have you watch your baby girl come through.

Love,
The Girl You Never Had xoxoxo

The End

I want to thank my family who saw my strength and my gifts. Nothing means more to me than you all and your happiness. My mother (Nette), Frank, Shaquelia, Anthony (AJ). SIP JT & Bryan, Vicki, Dana Tiffany...

To my friend, thanks for being one.

Thank you Victor for my spare, you're the real MVP. ☺

Thank you Ashlee for taking this journey with me.

Thank you to my *StyleRich* team.

If your dream was a butterfly remember you have to go through phases, stages and completion before you reach your "goal."